BREEDERS' BEST
A KENNEL CLUB BOOK™

Boxer

By Richard Tomita

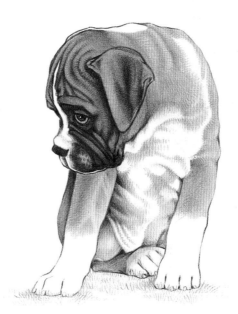

BREEDERS' BEST
A KENNEL CLUB BOOK™

BOXER

ISBN: 1-59378-904-1

Copyright © 2004

Kennel Club Books, LLC
308 Main Street, Allenhurst, NJ 07711 USA
Printed in South Korea

PHOTOS BY:
Isabelle Français,
Carol Ann Johnson,
Becky Lyn Tegze,
Siegi Lehmann
and Bernd Brinkmann.

DRAWINGS BY:
Yolyanko el Habanero

Contents

Meet the Boxer

To understand the history of the Boxer, one must travel centuries back in time to 2000 B.C. to the country of Epirus, known today as Albania, and the city of Molossis.

Author Rick Tomita with his housedog Kepler, a handsome example of a well-bred male adult.

The dogs of ancient Molossis were descendants of a legendary strain of dogs bred by the Assyrians. Known as Molossians, these dogs had heavy heads, powerful builds and great courage, and they were used as warriors in battle. The dogs spread across the Continent and

became the ancestors of the *Bullen-beisser* (German for "Bulldog" or "Bullbiter"), a large Mastiff-type dog, which evolved into the Boxer we know today.

A famous rendering of the ancestor of all mastiff breeds, the Molossian, drawn by Reinagle and published in 1803.

During their migration across Europe, three types and sizes of the Bullenbeisser emerged, although all were strongly built with similar head types, powerful muzzles and drooping upper lips. Early literature and paintings portray all Bullenbeissers as fawn- or brindle-colored with black masks.

Historians accept that a smaller type of Bullenbeisser bred in the Brabant area of Belgium is a direct ancestor of today's Boxer. One 18th-century writer tells of a Brabant Bullenbeisser with ears and tail that were clipped while the dog was still young. Early literature and artwork portray the dog bearing the trademark black mask and a fawn- or brindle-colored coat.

The Boxer is an active, medium-sized dog used for guardian and protection work.

The Germans used the smaller Bullenbeisser primarily as a hunting dog. John Wagner's historical reference describes the Bullenbeisser as a brilliant hunter: *"The Doggen and Bullenbeisser knew instinctively how to tackle game from behind and hold it in such a way that kept them from serious injury, yet gave the*

Schutzhund training includes sleeve work, where the Boxer's bite and brute strength are key to his success.

hunter time to reach the kill. Therefore they were more valuable to the hunt than other types of dogs and were highly prized and painstakingly bred."

The Bullenbeisser lived and worked on the estates of the German nobility. They were worked in packs, hunting wild bull, boar and small bear. When the Napoleonic wars ruptured the German hierarchy and dissolved their properties, the dogs were distributed among the peasants, the butchers and the cattle dealers who might best use their talents. The Bullenbeisser's intelligence, loyalty and trainability captivated the common folk, and by the late 1800s, these dogs had evolved into treasured family guard dogs and companions.

Prior to the Bullenbeisser, various types of dogs existed throughout Germany, but there were no breeding programs dedicated to a specific breed or type. In the 1880s, Boxer-type dogs were bred to taller, more elegant English imports, and those offspring became the forerunners of the modern Boxer. There is no record of how the name "Boxer" evolved from "Bullenbeisser," although some believe it stems from the breed's habit of rearing up and jabbing with its front paws during dog fights.

The first Boxer Club was

The Boxer was imported to the United States after World War I and was recognized by the American Kennel Club in 1904. The breed's

A white puppy in a litter of Boxers points to the breed's early bulldog ancestors.

formed in Munich in 1895, and the founders drew up a standard as a guide for future breeding programs. The careful genetic selection process utilized by the German breeders in their breeding programs over a century ago preserved those sterling qualities so treasured in the 21st-century Boxer.

work history as a pack dog placed him naturally in the AKC Working Group of dogs.

The Boxer's elegant chiseled head and stately silhouette dazzled the American dog fancier. His superior intelligence and easy-going, affectionate nature made him a favorite as a family dog. Boxer popularity hit a peak during the late 1940s and early 1950s, then suffered a decline. The breed has gained new ground in recent years, and today the Boxer ranks in the top ten in AKC registrations with over 37,000 registered.

The modern Boxer is a medium-sized dog, with males ranging from 65 to 80 pounds, females about 15 pounds less. Males can reach a height of 25 inches or more at the shoulder, females

Boxers have served in both World Wars as messenger dogs and military assistants.

several inches shorter. His coat is most distinctive, with a white "tuxedo" front and a black mask covering his well-

padded muzzle. The breed's average lifespan is about 11 years.

The Boxer's hearing is most acute, a sense that is enhanced by his erect, cropped ears, which makes him an instinctive guard dog. He worked as a courier during war time, and has also served as a guide dog for the blind. He was a war dog used to search for people trapped in collapsed buildings and to locate wounded soldiers left behind in advancing or retreating situations.

Boxers are utilized as aides for the blind, deaf and physically disabled.

The Boxer adores his human family, especially the children, and is happiest when he is with them. He is playful and patient with children and watches over them like a self-appointed nanny. His self-assured, dignified bearing makes him an excellent family guardian. While not aggressive, he is deliberate and discerning of strangers,

In times of crisis and war, the Boxer has served man in many capacities, including as a search and rescue helper.

and fearless if he or his loved ones are threatened. Boxer owners agree that this noble dog is the perfect combination of gentle protector and loving family member.

MEET THE BOXER

Overview

- From the line of ancient Molossians, the Boxer is the direct descendant of the Bullenbeissers of Belgium.
- The Germans promoted the breed and named it the "Boxer."
- The Americans are credited for refining the breed into the dazzling show dog and devoted family dog it is today.
- The Boxer's many talents and trainability have enabled him to assist man in various capacities, including as an assistant dog for the disabled, a messenger and war dog, and a search and rescue dog.

Description of the Boxer

The dapper gentleman Boxer you see gaiting merrily around the show ring is not an accident of birth. He is the product of decades of careful breeding practices, practices that followed the goals and dreams of the German breeders who founded the first Boxer Club over one hundred years ago.

In order to preserve the Boxer type they cherished for its exceptional good looks and amiable temperament, those breeders set forth a standard, a set of guidelines that described the ideal Boxer. Without such a guide, those

Responsible breeders aim to meet the qualifications described in the breed standard.

distinguishing features could be diluted through poor or irresponsible breeding practices and possibly lost forever.

Perhaps the first paragraph of the Boxer standard best captures the total essence of the breed. According to the standard: *The ideal Boxer is a medium-sized, square built dog of good substance with a short back, strong limbs and a short tight-fitting coat. Because he was developed to serve as a guard, working and companion dog, he should combine strength and agility with elegance and style. His expression is alert and his temperament is steadfast and tractable.*

Boxers are known for their handsome appearances, noble expressions and friendly temperaments.

"Medium size" means adult male Boxers stand 22.5 to 26 inches at the withers (top of the shoulder), and females 21 to 24 inches. The body is described as "square," which is in keeping with the Boxer's square-jawed head and overall appearance. Muscular, with a wide, deep chest, the body presents a commanding air of dignity and power.

The natural drop ears on the Boxer impart a peaceable, friendly impression.

CHAPTER 2

The breed's intelligence, loyalty and affection can be read in the Boxer's eyes.

Although the standard states that general appearance is to be given first consideration, there is much emphasis placed on the Boxer's handsome, chiseled head, which so distinguishes the breed from other similar types. His unique, chiseled head with its broad, blunt muzzle is his most distinctive feature, and *"great value is placed upon its being of proper form and balance with the skull."* Unlike that of the majority of other dog breeds, the Boxer's bite is undershot, with the lower jaw protruding beyond the upper and curving slightly inward. That distinctive bite is an important feature of the powerful Boxer head. The wide, square-jawed muzzle, being playfully pouty, also contributes to the trademark Boxer expression.

The Boxer's eyes are said to be "mood-mirroring," with the wrinkled forehead lending a unique and penetrating expression. One cannot meet the Boxer and not be mesmerized by his deep and soulful eyes. The ears are described as cropped, cut

The Boxer's muzzle must be correctly formed and properly balanced with the skull.

rather long and tapering, and raised when alert. Many breeders are asked by new owners to leave the ears natural. Ear cropping is forbidden in the UK and other countries in Europe.

The Boxer coat is short and shiny, lying smooth and tight to the body. The breed colors are fawn and brindle, with fawn shades varying

Boxer

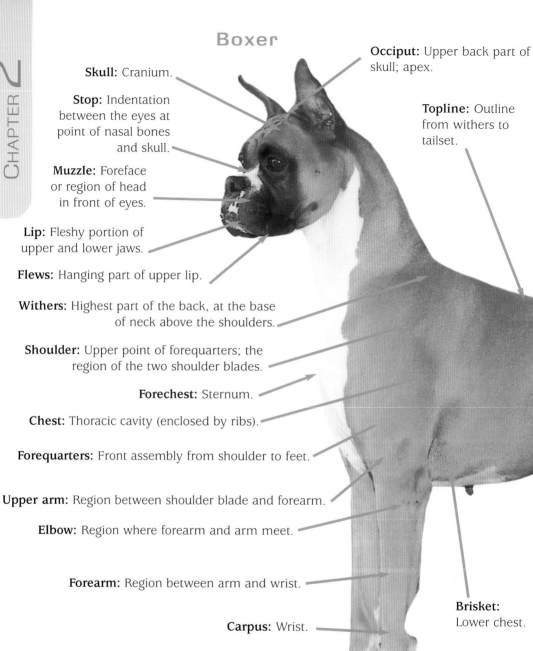

Skull: Cranium.

Occiput: Upper back part of skull; apex.

Stop: Indentation between the eyes at point of nasal bones and skull.

Topline: Outline from withers to tailset.

Muzzle: Foreface or region of head in front of eyes.

Lip: Fleshy portion of upper and lower jaws.

Flews: Hanging part of upper lip.

Withers: Highest part of the back, at the base of neck above the shoulders.

Shoulder: Upper point of forequarters; the region of the two shoulder blades.

Forechest: Sternum.

Chest: Thoracic cavity (enclosed by ribs).

Forequarters: Front assembly from shoulder to feet.

Upper arm: Region between shoulder blade and forearm.

Elbow: Region where forearm and arm meet.

Forearm: Region between arm and wrist.

Brisket: Lower chest.

Carpus: Wrist.

Dewclaw: Extra digit on inside leg; fifth toe.

Pastern: Region between wrist and toes.

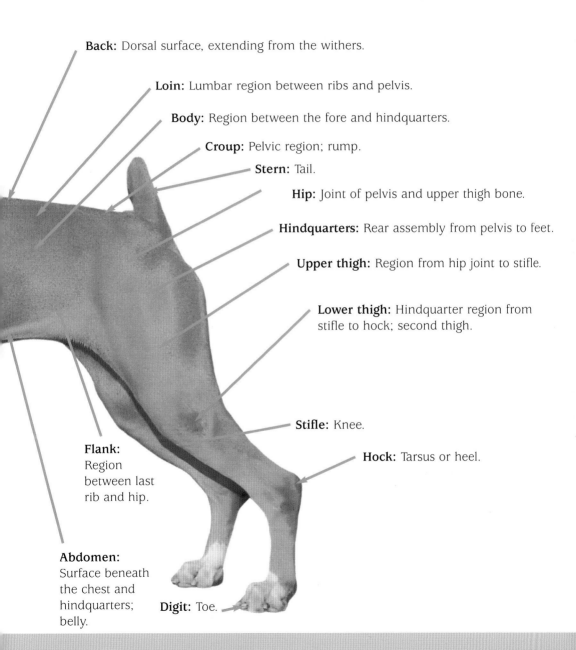

Back: Dorsal surface, extending from the withers.

Loin: Lumbar region between ribs and pelvis.

Body: Region between the fore and hindquarters.

Croup: Pelvic region; rump.

Stern: Tail.

Hip: Joint of pelvis and upper thigh bone.

Hindquarters: Rear assembly from pelvis to feet.

Upper thigh: Region from hip joint to stifle.

Lower thigh: Hindquarter region from stifle to hock; second thigh.

Stifle: Knee.

Hock: Tarsus or heel.

Flank: Region between last rib and hip.

Abdomen: Surface beneath the chest and hindquarters; belly.

Digit: Toe.

from light tan to stag red. The brindle can range from sparse but clearly defined black herringbone pattern on a fawn background to such a heavy concentration of black striping that it almost totally masks the fawn background color. White markings are desired for show but may not exceed one-third of the entire coat. White on the face may replace part of the mask and extend upward between the eyes, but should not be excessive. Colors other than fawn or brindle or excessive white markings (exceeding

Champion Jacquet's Grimthrope, known as "Clifford" to his friends, is an excellent example of a brindle male. Clifford has a gorgeous headpiece and a desirably square, muscular body.

one-third of the entire coat) are disqualifying faults.

The standard describes character and temperament as *of paramount importance,* and a prospective Boxer owner would do well to understand the Boxer's unique personality. He is instinctively a hearing guard dog, and his bearing is alert, dignified and self-assured. In the show ring, he should exhibit constrained animation. With family and friends, his temperament is fundamentally playful, yet

Bitches may be more affectionate than dogs, though both are courageous and loyal.

patient and tolerant with children. Deliberate and wary with strangers, he will exhibit curiosity but, most importantly, fearless courage if threatened. However, he responds to friendly overtures honestly rendered. His intelligence, loyal affection and tractability to discipline make him a highly desirable companion. A lack of dignity, alertness or shyness are noted faults.

A thorough understanding of the Boxer standard will prepare potential owners for this ideal companion for the family.

Brindling can appear as heavy concentration of black striping that it nearly masks the fawn background.

A DESCRIPTION OF THE BOXER

Overview

- The breed standard, devised by the parent club, describes the ideal Boxer, detailing both physical conformation as well as character and movement.
- The Boxer's body should appear "square," muscular with a deep, wide chest.
- The head, a most prominent feature, is chiseled with a broad, blunt muzzle. The bite is undershot.
- The coat is short and lies smooth, colored in fawn or brindle with or without white markings.

Are You a Boxer Person?

The Boxer never fails to impress his audience, whether trotting in the show ring or walking in the neighborhood. His regal bearing and striking silhouette naturally command the respect and admiration of experienced dog fanciers as well as ordinary dog lovers. It is said to know one is to love one. However, if you want to own a Boxer, you should definitely have an in-depth knowledge of the breed before you add one to your family.

Despite his famous tuxedoed

To know a Boxer is to love a Boxer.

silhouette, the Boxer's most notable characteristic is his highly affectionate nature. He is a "people" dog who is happiest when he is with his human family. He is playful with his own family and known for his stoic patience when playing with children.

Boxer puppies adore the company of children.

Although a medium-sized breed, the male Boxer weighs 65 to 80 pounds and is considered large by some. The adult Boxer is neither nervous nor hyper-active. He can be rambunctious as a youngster, and thus needs training and supervision. Boxers are very trainable, but are known to harbor a stubborn streak. Early training from puppyhood and beyond is essential to a healthy relationship between the Boxer and his master. He needs to learn at an early age who is in charge or he will assume that role himself. A natural guard dog, he needs obedience instruction to channel his protective instincts into a safe demeanor. These needs should be addressed before

Applause, applause for a handsome, trotting show Boxer. This is International Champion Jacquet's Destino El Encanto.

you decide to bring a Boxer puppy home. Are you ready to assume these duties?

The Boxer coat is relatively care-free and requires little maintenance other than a weekly brushing to keep it clean

Male Boxers can weigh 15 pounds more than their female counterparts.

and shining. The balance of good grooming still takes time…nail trimming, ear and teeth cleaning…all prerequisites for a healthy dog of any breed.

The Boxer needs a fenced-in yard for safe exercise and play. The Boxer should never be allowed to run loose for any reason. A loose Boxer is a danger to himself and to other people who may regard him as a threat. Invisible electrical fences can work well if the dog is properly trained to observe the boundaries and wears the battery-powered collar. However, such fences offer no protection from strange dogs, children or other intruders who can come into the yard, so outside play still must be supervised. Furthermore, invisible fences do not provide a physical barrier or buffer between the dog and kids on bikes, passing cars, squirrels and other moving attractions. Such stimuli can arouse the dog into testing the limits of the fence and getting shocked, which will condition him to associate the pain with the objects he is focused on at the time. Thus, those situations will come to cause frustration and escalating aggressive behaviors. On-leash walks are the best answer for safe daily exercise for your fun-loving Boxer.

Discuss electrical fences with the breeder of your choice. He may be able to advise you of his success (or disappointment) with such a device. If used properly in the right setting, the electrical fence can be effective and helpful (and far less expensive than erecting a conventional fence). Safety is the Boxer person's first priority.

Boxers are friendly and happy dogs.

ARE YOU A BOXER PERSON?

Overview

- The Boxer person is ready and able to assume a leadership role with the intelligent, sometimes stubborn Boxer, a breed designed for protection work and guard duty.
- The Boxer person has time to exercise and care for the dog and can provide ample accommodations.
- The Boxer person is responsible and available, for this breed makes its highly affectionate ways known to the ones it chooses to call its own.
- The Boxer person makes certain that his dog is safe at all times.

Selecting a Boxer Breeder

A reputable breeder is the only source for a quality Boxer pup. Whatever your reason for wanting a Boxer pup— companionship, dog shows or obedience competition—you want a healthy dog with an excellent tempera- ment. Avoid for-profit operations that care only about the bottom- line dollar and not about the health and stability of the dogs they mass-produce. Only a responsible breeder can provide a healthy pup that is well suited to your lifestyle and long-term goals. Good

Meeting the dam of the litter provides the owner with critical information about the puppies. Pup are usually weaned by the time visitors arrive.

breeders know the puppies they sell.

Locating a good breeder can be an emotionally trying experience, taxing your patience and your willpower. All puppies are adorable and it's easy to fall in love with the first cute pup you see, but a poorly bred Boxer will have health and temperament problems that can empty your wallet and break your heart. Do your breeder homework before you visit litters. Arm yourself with a list of questions for the breeder. A good breeder will expect that. Then leave your checkbook and your kids at home so you aren't tempted to take home a poorly bred but nonetheless irresistible Boxer pup.

A litter of typical brindle puppies bred by author Richard Tomita of the Jacquet Boxers.

For starters, ask to see the pedigree and American Kennel Club (AKC) registration papers. The pedigree should include three to five generations of ancestry. Inquire about any titles in the pedigree. Titles simply indicate a dog's accomplishments in

The breeder should be as friendly and outgoing as the puppies.

some area of canine competition, proving the merits of his ancestors and adding to the breeder's credibility. Examples are "Ch." for the show title of Champion, "CD" for the obedience title of Companion Dog and "SchH. I" for the working Schutzhund title. While it is true that a pedigree is no guarantee of health or breed quality, it is still a good sign of a serious breeder.

A show puppy will have the structure and attitude of a future star.

Ask the breeder why he planned this litter. A good breeder should explain the genetics behind this particular breeding and what he expects the breeding to produce. He never breeds because "his Boxer is sweet and/or beautiful, his neighbor's dog

is handsome, they will have lovely puppies," and so on. Just loving his dog like crazy does not qualify an individual to breed dogs intelligently or to properly raise a litter of Boxer pups.

Ask about health clearances. Boxers are prone to hip dysplasia, thyroid disease and heart defects. Cardiomyopathy and aortic/subaortic valvular stenosis are two serious heart conditions that can result in sudden and unexpected death in both young and adult Boxers. The only way to produce puppies that are not affected with these genetic diseases is for a veterinarian to test the parents and certify them as free of these defects before they are bred. Have the parents been screened for heart problems by a board-certified veterinary cardiologist?

Ask the breeder if the sire and dam have hip clearances from OFA (Orthopedic

Foundation for Animals, a national canine hip registry). Has the breeder had thyroid testing done on the sire and dam? Good breeders will gladly, in fact *proudly*, provide those documents. For more information on genetic disease in Boxers, you can check out the American Boxer Club website at americanboxerclub.org.

The breeder should also explain that Boxers are also prone to a condition called bloat (gastric dilatation/volvulus). This is a life-threatening condition that is common in deep-chested breeds such as the Boxer, Weimaraner, Bloodhound, Great Dane and other similarly constructed breeds. Bloat occurs when the stomach fills rapidly with air and begins to twist, cutting off the blood supply. If not treated immediately, the dog will die.

Experienced breeders are frequently involved in some

aspect of the dog fancy with their dog(s), perhaps showing or training them for some type of performance event or dog-related activity. Their

Even a young pup will be solidly constructed with no signs of limping or other physical defects.

Boxer(s) may have earned titles in various canine competitions, which is added proof of their experience and commitment to the breed.

Dedicated breeders who are truly involved with their dogs usually belong to the American Boxer Club and perhaps a local breed or kennel club. Such affiliation with other experienced breeders and fanciers expands their knowledge of the breed and breed characteristics, which further enhances a breeder's credi-

A white pup can make a terrific pet, though will not be eligible for showing or breeding.

bility. Responsible breeders, by the way, do not raise many different breeds of dog or produce multiple litters of pups throughout the year; one or two litters a year is typical for a small breeder. There are some notable exceptions, and their walls are adorned with hundreds of blue ribbons and championship certificates.

The breeder will ask you questions too…about your dog history, about previous dogs you have owned, what breeds of dog and what became of these dogs. He will want to know your living arrangements, i.e., house, yard, kids, etc., your goals for this pup and how you plan to raise him. The breeder's primary concern is the future of the puppies and whether you and your family are suitable owners who will provide proper and loving homes for his precious little one. Avoid any breeder who agrees to sell you a puppy without any type of interrogation process. Such indifference indicates a lack of concern about the pups, and casts doubt on the breeder's ethics and his breeding program.

A good breeder will tell you about the character of the Boxer and what to expect and

The Orthopedic Foundation for Animals (OFA) was founded by John M. Olin and a group of caring veterinarians and dog breeders in the mid-1960s. The goal of the new foundation was to provide x-ray evaluations and guidance to dog breeders with regard to hip dysplasia, a common hereditary disease that affects many different breeds of dog.

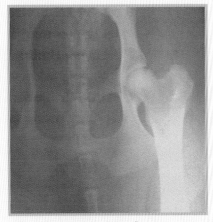

X-ray of a dog with "Good" hips.

Three board-certified OFA radiologists evaluate x-rays of dogs that are 24 months of age or older, scoring their hips as "Excellent," "Good" and "Fair," all of which are eligible for breeding. Dogs that score "Borderline," "Mild," "Moderate" and "Severe" are not eligible for breeding. The sire and dam of your new puppy should have OFA numbers, proving that they are eligible for breeding.

Since OFA's inception, the organization has expanded to include databases on elbow dysplasia, patellar luxation, autoimmune thyroiditis, congenital heart disease, Legg-Calve-Perthes disease, sebaceous adenitis, congenital deafness, craniomandibular osteopathy, von Willebrand's disease, copper toxicosis, cystinuria, renal dysplasia and other diseases that have hereditary bases in dogs.

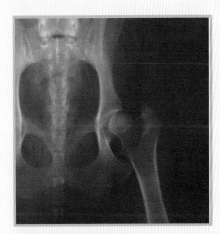

X-ray of a dog with "Moderate" dysplastic hips.

Visit the OFA website for more information on the organization, its history, its goals and the diseases from which it safeguards our pure-bred dogs. Go to www.offa.com.

Healthy, responsive and intelligent—the only puppy to buy.

whether the Boxer will fit your lifestyle. Be prepared to weigh the good news against the not so good news about the Boxer.

Most Boxer breeders have a puppy sales contract that includes specific health guarantees and reasonable return policies. They should agree to accept a puppy back if it does not work out. They also should be willing, indeed anxious, to check up on the puppy's progress after the

Are you ready to provide a loving home to a new Boxer puppy?

pup leaves the breeder's home, and be available if you have questions or problems with the pup.

Many breeders place their pet puppies on what is called the AKC Limited Registration. This does register the pup with AKC, but does not allow the registration of any offspring from the mature dog. *Pet dogs should not be bred.* The breeder, and only the breeder, can cancel the Limited Registration if the adult dog develops into breeding quality.

If you have any doubts at all, feel free to ask for references...and check them out. It's unlikely a breeder will offer names of unhappy

puppy clients, but any bit of information you can glean will make you more comfortable dealing with a particular breeder.

You can expect to pay a fair price for all of these breeder qualities, whether you fancy a pet Boxer for a companion dog, or one with show or obedience potential. The discount or bargain Boxer is not a bargain at all. Indeed, the discount pup is in reality a potential disaster that may have little chance of developing into a healthy, stable adult. Such bargains could ultimately cost you a fortune in vet expenses and heartache that can't be measured in dollars and cents.

So how do you find a reputable breeder you can trust? Do your puppy homework before you visit litters. Ask your veterinarian or, if you don't have one, ask a friend's vet for a referral. Spend the day at a dog show or other dog event where you

can meet breeders and exhibitors and get to know their dogs. Most Boxer fanciers are more than happy to show off their dogs and

Good breeders will know their dogs for four or five generations, and are willing to share photos and records of all of your puppy's ancestors. Here's William Scolnik with Jacquet's Kepler.

brag about their accomplishments. If you know a Boxer you are fond of, ask the owner where he got his dog. Ask him to recommend a breeder.

The breeder has begun the socialization of the puppies, and produced friendly, happy "kids" who enjoy the company of humans.

Check with the American Kennel Club for breeder referrals in your area. Their website (www.akc.org) offers links to breed clubs and breeder referrals throughout the United States.

Skip the puppy ads in your local paper. Reputable breeders rarely advertise in newspapers. They are very particular about prospective puppy owners and do not rely on mass advertising to attract the right people. Rather, they depend on referrals from other breeders and previous puppy clients. They also are more than willing to keep any puppy past the seven- or eight-week placement age until the right person comes along.

Perhaps the second most important ingredient in your breeder search is patience. You will not likely find the right breeder or litter on your first go-around. Breeders often have waiting lists, but a good Boxer pup is worth the wait. The time and effort you invest at this point in time will pay off tenfold in the future.

SELECTING A BOXER BREEDER

Overview

- To find a reputable breeder, write or phone the American Kennel Club or the American Boxer Club for contacts.
- Visit a dog show to meet breeders and handlers of good dogs.
- Know what to expect from a quality breeder and be patient in your search.
- Ask about pedigrees, sales agreements, health clearances, registration papers and references.
- The breeder should inform you about the incidence of hip dysplasia, cancer, hypothyroidism and other hereditary conditions in his line.

Finding the Right Puppy

S electing the right puppy is as important as finding a good breeder. Once you find a breeder you can trust, it's time to visit the puppies to decide if this litter is right for you. The perfect pup is seldom right around the corner, and you may have to travel to visit a good litter. Up close and personal is the only way to choose your pup. That way, you can become better acquainted with the breeder, the dam of the pups and the environment in which the pups were raised. If possible, visit more than one

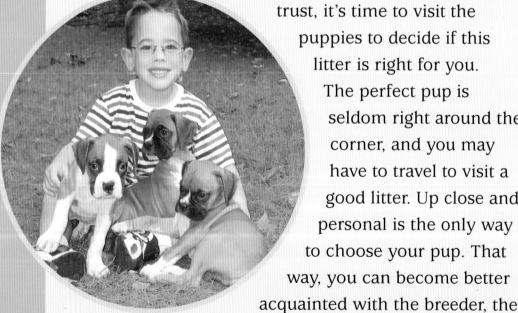

After you've determined that you've found a quality litter, allow the child to participate in the selection.

litter and keep notes on what you see and like…and don't like…about each one. Your research will pay off.

Where and how a litter of pups is raised is vitally important to their early development into confident, social pups. The litter should be kept in the house, indoors or in an adjoining sheltered area, not isolated in a basement, garage or outside barn. Boxer puppies need to be socialized daily with people and people activities. The greater their exposure to everyday sights and sounds, the easier their adjustment to their future human family.

That the litter is raised with love is the most important criteria when selecting from a healthy brood.

During your visit, scrutinize the puppies as well as their living area for cleanliness and signs of sickness or poor health. The pups should be reasonably clean (allowing for normal non-stop "puppy-pies"). They should appear energetic, bright-eyed and alert. Healthy pups have clean, thick coats, are well proportioned and feel

Meeting the breeder, dam and puppy is critical in order to make a good selection.

solid and muscular without being overly fat or pot-bellied. Watch for crusted eyes or nose and any watery discharge from the nose, eyes or ears. Check for evidence of watery or bloody stools.

Visit with the dam and the sire if possible. In many cases, the sire is not on the premises, but the breeder should have photos and a résumé of his accomplish-

Check the bite of your potential puppy. The Boxer's bite should be undershot, meaning the lower jaw protrudes slightly from the upper.

ments. It is normal for some dams to be protective of their young, but overly aggressive behavior is unacceptable. Temperament is inherited, and if one or both parents are aggressive or shy, it is likely that some of the pups might inherit those characteristics.

Notice how the pups interact with their littermates and their surroundings, especially their response to people. They should be active and outgoing. In many Boxer litters, some pups will be more outgoing than others, but even a quiet pup that is properly socialized should not be shy or spooky or shrink from a friendly voice or outstretched hand.

The breeder should be honest in discussing any differences in puppy personalities. Although most breeders do some type of temperament testing, they also have spent most of the past seven or eight weeks cuddling and cleaning up after these pups. By this point in time, they should know the subtle differences in each pup's personality. The breeder's observations are valuable aids in selecting a puppy that will be compatible with you and your lifestyle.

Tell the breeder if you plan

to show your pup in conformation or compete in other
events or field-related activities. Some pups will show
more promise than others,
and he can help you select
one that will best suit your
long-term goals.

Do you prefer a male or
female? Which one is right for
you? Both sexes are loving and
loyal, and the differences are
due to individual personalities
more than gender. The Boxer
female is a gentle soul and
easy to live with, but she also
can be a bit more moody or
frivolous, depending on her
whims and hormonal peaks.

The male is often up to 2
inches taller than the female
and is bigger and more
powerful. Although males
tend to be more loyal to the
family than bitches, they can
be more physical and
exuberant during adoles-
cence, which can be
problematic in a rather large
and powerful dog. An
untrained male can become

dominant with other males
and sometimes with people
they don't know. A solid
foundation in obedience is
necessary if you want your
dog to respect you as his
leader.

A well-socialized litter will welcome visitors with ease, and enthusiasm.

Intact males tend to be
more territorial, especially
with other male dogs.
Neutering your male and
spaying your female Boxer
will create a level playing field
and eliminate most of these
gender-related differences.
Many vets feel that your
Boxer will live longer, too.
What better reason to spay
and neuter?

By seven weeks, the pups should have had at least one worming and a first puppy shot, and have a vet certificate verifying that he is in good health at the time of the exam. Tails should have been docked within a few days of birth, and front dewclaws removed at the same time. In males, both testicles should be descended into the scrotum. A dog with undescended testicles will make a fine pet, but will be ineligible for the show ring.

Post-surgical ear care includes taping the ears to set them into place.

The Boxer's erect and pointed ears are one of the distinguishing features of the breed. Ear cropping is believed to be appropriate for the well-being of the breed, as the upright ear minimizes the potential for the ear infections that plague many flop-eared breeds. However, ear cropping has become the subject of international controversy, and the practice is now banned as unnecessary in Britain, Australia and Scandinavia. Breeders and owners in other countries also disapprove of ear cropping and prefer to leave their Boxer's ears natural and floppy. Dissenting breeders do not believe the procedure causes pain.

Cropping, if done, is performed under general anesthesia, usually between six and nine weeks of age. The breeder will provide after-care instructions and taping if the ears are not yet standing upright.

The breeder should tell you what the pup has been eating, when and how much. Some send home an ample supply of puppy food to start his client off for the first few days. Most breeders also give their clients a puppy "take-home" packet, which includes a copy of the health certificate, the puppy's pedigree and registration papers, copies of the parents' health clearances and the breeder's sales contract. Many breeders supply literature on the breed and how to properly raise and train a

Whether you choose a male or female puppy, you will have a loving companion for life.

Boxer. Dedicated breeders know that the more you know, the better life will be for their precious Boxer pups. If you're really lucky, they gave you a copy of this book!

FINDING THE RIGHT PUPPY

Overview

- Visit the litter to see the puppies firsthand. You are seeking healthy, sound puppies. "Cute" is not a qualification, though bright eyes, shiny coats and solid little frames count for a lot.
- Trust the breeder whom you've selected to recommend a puppy that fits your lifestyle and personality.
- Decide upon a male or a female puppy based on gender-related personality and physical differences.
- Decide whether you want a cropped- or natural-eared pup.
- If you intend to show, discuss this with the breeder.

Welcoming the Boxer

Your puppy's home-coming is a major event in his brief puppy life. How you handle the big occasion will help him make a pleasant adjustment to a new world without his mom and littermates.

You need to puppy-proof the house and stock up on puppy supplies before your pup comes home. You won't have time after he arrives. A thorough puppy-proofing will prevent any accidents or surprises that could be dangerous or even fatal for your pup. It also will preserve your property and your peace of mind.

Welcoming the puppy is an exciting time.

Puppy shopping is the fun part, but hang on to your purse strings. Puppy stuff, especially the non-essentials, is often too cute to resist, so "stocking up" can easily decimate your budget. Start with basic essentials, and save the puppy goodies until later.

PUPPY SHOPPING LIST
Puppy Food

Your Boxer pup should be fed a quality food that is appropriate for his age and breed. Most quality dog foods now offer breed-specific formulas that address the nutritional needs of small, medium (your Boxer) and large breeds of dog during the various stages of their lives. Boxers grow rapidly and need a well-balanced food to stay healthy during that first year of rapid growth. Buy a supply of medium-breed growth food, which should be his diet for his first year. After that, you can switch to a

Have a secure site for the location of your dog house. The dog house must last for many years

The ideal family dog—here's Chowder with siblings Zack and Grace, members of the extended Jacquet Boxer family.

medium-breed adult-maintenance food.

Your Boxer's early growth period as well as his long-term health will benefit from a diet of high-quality puppy and dog food. For recommendations based on experience, check with your breeder and your vet before you buy your puppy's food.

Select sturdy bowls for your Boxer, made of hard plastic or stainless steel.

Food and Water Bowls

You'll need two separate serving pieces, one for food and one for water. Stainless steel bowls are your best choice, as they are chew-proof and easy to clean. Boxers have powerful jaws and love to chew. Aluminum and plastic are much too flimsy, and those cute ceramic bowls break easily. Tip-proof is a good idea, since most puppies love to splash about in their water bowls, and the Boxer pup is no exception. Bowl stands for the adolescent and adult Boxer are a must.

Collars and ID Tags

Your Boxer pup should have an adjustable collar that will expand to fit him as he grows. Lightweight nylon adjustable collars work best for both pups and adult dogs. To fit properly, you should be able to slip two fingers between the collar and your puppy's neck. The ID tag should have your phone number, name and address, but *not* the puppy's name, as that would enable a stranger to identify and call your dog. Some owners include a line that says "Dog needs medication," intended to speed the dog's return if he is lost or stolen. Put the collar

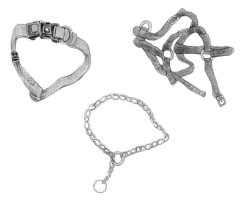

Three choices for collars. Clockwise from upper right: halter, chain choke collar and the traditional buckle collar.

on as soon the pup comes home so he can get used to wearing it. It's best to use an "O" ring for the tag, as the "S" ring snags on carpets and comes off easily.

Today, even dog collars have gone high-tech. Some come equipped with beepers and tracking devices. The most advanced pet identification tool uses a Global Positioning System and fits inside a collar or tag. When your dog leaves his programmed home perimeter, the device sends a message directly to your phone or e-mail address.

Choke collars are for training purposes and should be worn only during training ses-

sions. Training collars should never be used on Boxer puppies under 16 weeks of age.

Leashes

For your own convenience and for the puppy's safety, his leash wardrobe should include at least two kinds of leads. A narrow six-foot leather leash is best for walks, puppy kindergarten, obedience class and leash-training workouts. The other lead is the flexible lead. "Flexis" are extendable leads, housed in a large handle, which extend and retract with the push of a button. This is the ideal tool for exercising and should be a staple in every puppy's wardrobe. Flexible leads are available in

Teach your Boxer that his leash doesn't count among his chew toys.

several lengths (8 feet to 26 feet) and strengths, depending on breed size. Longer is better, as it allows your dog to run about and check out the good sniffing areas farther away from you. They are especially handy for exercising your puppy in unfenced areas or when traveling with your dog. You must train your Boxer to the flexible lead as a pup because an untrained adult Boxer may be too much to handle on a "Flexi."

For transportation and training, crates are a must for all puppy owners.

Bedding

Dog beds are just plain fun. Beds run the gamut from small and inexpensive to elegant, high-end beds suitable for the most royal of dog breeds. However, don't go overboard just yet. Better to save that fancy bed for when your Boxer is older and less apt to shred it up or make a puddle on it. For puppy bedding, it's best to use a large towel, mat or blanket that can be easily laundered (which will probably be often).

Crating and Gating

These will be your most important puppy purchases. A crate is *your* most valuable tool for housebreaking your pup, and *his* favorite place to feel secure. Crates come in three varieties: wire mesh, fabric mesh, and the more familiar plastic, airline-type crate. Wire or fabric crates offer the best ventilation and some conveniently fold up suitcase-style. A mesh-fabric crate might be a little risky for the Boxer youngster who likes to dig and chew. Whatever your choice, purchase an adult-size crate, about 20 x 30 inches, rather than a small or puppy size; your Boxer pup will soon grow into the adult size. Crates are available at most pet stores.

Rubber balls are ideal for playing and chasing.

A well-placed baby gate will protect your house from the inevitable puppy mischief, and thus save your sanity as well. It's wise to confine puppy to a tiled or uncarpeted room or space, one that is accessible to the outside door he will use for potty trips. Gated to a safe area where he cannot wreak havoc or destruction, your puppy will soon learn to chew only appropriate toys and spare himself unnecessary corrections for normal puppy mishaps. Gated, however, does not mean unsupervised. Boxer puppies are active and exuberant, and require attention and activity to keep them out of mischief. If he must be unattended, use his crate.

Toys

Filling your Boxer puppy's toybox is terrific fun, but can be expensive. Visit your local pet shop to see a wide array of dog toys. Purchase one or two different types of toys, one for chewing (like a rawhide chew or plastic bone) and one for playing and chasing (like a flying disk, ball or squeaky toy). As always, safety is the most important factor when shopping for

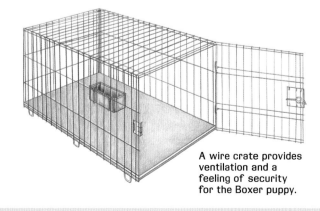

A wire crate provides ventilation and a feeling of security for the Boxer puppy.

CHAPTER 6

your pup's toys. Avoid toys with small pieces that can break off and be swallowed. Natural bones, likewise, can be problematic unless you can supervise your Boxer whenever he's playing with a real bone.

There is a wide selection of dog toys waiting for you and your Boxer at your local pet-supply store. Bring your Boxer along to make a selection.

Grooming Tools

Boxers are considered easy keepers. You don't need a battery of combs and brushes to keep them tidy. A slicker brush and a grooming glove are the only implements needed to maintain a clean and shiny coat. Introduce your puppy to grooming with a soft bristle brush early on so he learns to like it. It also helps condition the pup to hands-on attention, which will be invaluable when you have to clean his teeth and ears, and clip his nails.

SOCIALIZATION

This actually puppy-proofs your puppy, not your house. Puppy socialization is your Boxer's insurance policy for happy, stable adulthood and is, without question, the most important element in a Boxer puppy's introduction to the human world. Boxers tend to appoint themselves guardians of their households. Thus, it is most important to expose them to strangers and new situations at an early age. It has been proven that unsocialized pups, especially those with guardian instincts like the Boxer, grow up to be spooky and insecure, and fearful of people, children and strange places. Many turn into fear biters or become aggressive with other dogs, strangers, even family members. Such dogs can seldom be rehabilitated and often end up abandoned in animal shelters where they are ultimately euthanized. Puppy socialization lays the foundation for a well-behaved adult canine, thus preventing those canine behaviors that lead to abandonment and euthanasia.

The primary socialization period occurs during puppy's first 20 weeks of life. Once he leaves the safety of his mom and littermates at seven to ten weeks of age, your job begins. Start with a quiet, uncomplicated household for the first day or two, and then gradually introduce him to the sights and sounds of his new human world. Frequent interaction with children, new people and other dogs are essential at this age. Visit new places (dog-friendly, of course) like parks or even the local mall where there are crowds of people. Set each

Puppy Safety at Home

After puppy shopping, you must puppy-proof your house. Boxer pups are naturally curious critters that will investigate everything new, then seek-and-destroy just because it's fun. The message here is..never let your puppy roam your house unsupervised. Scout your house for the following hazards:

Trash Cans and Diaper Pails
These are natural puppy magnets (they know where the good smelly stuff is!)

Medication Bottles, Cleaning Materials, Roach and Rodent Poisons
Lock these up. You'll be amazed at what a determined puppy can find.

Electrical Cords
Unplug wherever you can and make the others inaccessible. Injuries from chewed electrical cords are extremely common in young dogs.

Dental Floss, Yarn, Needles and Thread, and Other Stringy Stuff
Puppies snuffling about at ground level will find and ingest the tiniest of objects and will end up in surgery.

Toilet Bowl Cleaners
If you have them, throw them out now. All dogs are born with "toilet sonar" and quickly discover that the water there is always cold.

Garage
Beware of antifreeze! It is extremely toxic and even a few drops will kill an adult Boxer, less for a pup. Lock it and all other chemicals well out of reach. Fertilizers can also be toxic to dogs.

Socks and Underwear, Shoes and Slippers, Too
Keep them off the floor and close your closet doors. Puppies love all of the above because they smell like you times 10! Most vets can tell you stories about the stuff they surgically removed from a puppy's gut.

goal of two new places a week for the next two months. Keep these new situations upbeat and positive. This will create a positive attitude toward future encounters.

"Positive" is especially important when visiting your veterinarian. You don't want a pup that quakes with fear every time he sets a paw inside

Boxer puppies adore the company of children, but always supervise interaction to ensure positive experiences.

his doctor's office. Make sure your vet is a true dog lover as well as a dog doctor.

Your puppy also will need supervised exposure to children. Boxers are, by nature, good with children, but both

dog and child must learn how to behave properly with each other. Puppies of all breeds tend to view little people as littermates and will exert the upper paw (a dominance ploy) over the child. Boxers are large and happy dogs who could unintentionally overwhelm a small child during play. Children must be taught how to properly play with the dog and to respect his privacy. Likewise, adult family members should teach the puppy not to nip or jump up on the kids, and all puppy-child interactions should be supervised.

Take your Boxer youngster to puppy school. Some classes accept pups at ten weeks of age, with one series of puppy shots as a health requirement. The younger the pup, the easier it is to shape good behavior patterns. A good puppy class teaches proper canine social etiquette rather than rigid obedience skills. Your puppy will meet and play with young dogs of other breeds, and you will learn about the positive teaching tools you'll need to train your pup.

Puppy class is important for both novice and experienced puppy folks. If you're a smart Boxer owner, you won't stop there and will continue on with a basic obedience class. Of course, you want the best-behaved Boxer in the neighborhood!

Remember this: There is a direct correlation between the quality and amount of time you spend with your puppy during his first 20 weeks of life and the character of the adult dog he will become. You cannot recapture this valuable learning period, so make the most of it.

While it's great to keep your Boxer puppy busy with fun toys, you also must spend time with him. He wants to play with you!

WELCOMING THE BOXER

Overview

- Get your checkbook and go to the pet store! You're going to need food, bowls, a collar and ID tags, toys, a leash and collar, a crate, a brush and comb and more.
- Make your home safe for your puppy by removing hazards from the dog's environment.
- Socialization is critical to your puppy's proper development. Be proactive by introducing him to children and other dogs. Keep new experiences positive and fun.
- Try a puppy class as a way to socialize and train your new pup.

Boxer Puppy Kindergarten

Although the Boxer is an affectionate and highly intelligent dog, he also has a mind of his own. He needs to learn that you are now the top dog, the "alpha" person in his life. The sooner he understands that, the fewer behavior problems you will encounter with your puppy and adult Boxer.

All dogs are pack animals and, as such, they need a leader. Your Boxer's first boss was his mother, now it's *you*. How best to teach him that you are now the chief in his life? Puppy kindergarten starts the day you bring

The Boxer puppy is full of affection and ready to become a member of his new pack—yours!

your puppy home.

Before your puppy left his breeder, all of his life lessons came from his dam and littermates. When he played too rough or nipped too hard, his siblings cried and stopped the game. When he got pushy or obnoxious, his dam cuffed him gently with a maternal paw. Now his human family has to communicate appropriate behavior in terms his little canine mind will understand.

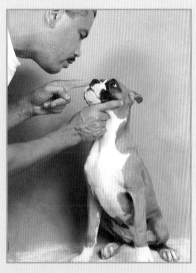

Make your intentions clearly known, but always be positive during lesson time.

When you start the teaching process, keep this thought uppermost: The first 20 weeks of any canine's life is his most valuable learning time, a period when his mind is best able to soak up every lesson, both positive and negative. Positive experiences and proper socialization during this period are critical to his future development and stability. Always keep in mind that the amount and quality of time you invest with your Boxer youngster now will determine what kind of an adult

Puppies wrestling to determine who is "top dog."

he will become. Wild dog or a gentleman or lady? Well-behaved or naughty dog? It's up to you.

Canine behavioral science tells us that any behavior that is rewarded will be repeated (this is called *positive reinforcement*). If something good happens, like a tasty treat or hugs and kisses, the

The earliest puppy training starts when the youngsters interact among themselves. They learn not to bite too hard as they mouth and nip at their littermates.

puppy will naturally want to repeat the behavior. That same research also has proven that one of the best ways to a puppy's mind is

through his stomach. *Never underestimate the power of a cookie!*

This leads to another very important puppy rule: Keep your pockets loaded with puppy treats at all times, so you are prepared to reinforce good behavior whenever it occurs.

That same reinforcement principle also applies to negative behavior, or what we humans (not the dog) might consider negative (like digging in the trash can, which the dog or puppy does not know is "wrong"). If the pup gets into the garbage, steals food or does anything else that makes him feel good, he will do it again. What better reason to keep a sharp eye on your puppy to prevent these normal canine behaviors?

PUPPY'S HOME EDUCATION

You are about to begin the puppy classes. There are two rules to consider. Rule

Number One: The puppy must learn that you are now the "alpha" dog and his new pack leader. Rule Number Two: You have to teach him in a manner he will understand (sorry, barking just won't do it). Remember, always, that he knows nothing about human standards of behavior.

Word Association

Use the same word (command) for each behavior every time you teach it, adding food rewards and verbal praise to reinforce the positive. The pup will make the connection and will be motivated to repeat the behavior when he hears those key words. For example, when teaching pup to potty outside, use the same potty command ("Go potty," "Get busy" or "Hurry up" are commonly used) each time he eliminates, adding a "Good boy!" while he's urinating or eliminating. Pup will soon learn what those trips outside are for.

Timing

All dogs learn their lessons in the present tense. You have to catch them in the act (good or bad) in order to dispense rewards or discipline. You have five seconds to connect with your dog or he will not

Playtime is vital in the development of your Boxer puppy.

understand what he did wrong. Thus, timing and consistency are your keys to success in teaching any new behavior or correcting bad behaviors.

Rules to Remember

Successful puppy training depends upon several important principles:

1. Use simple one-word commands and say them only once. Otherwise, the puppy learns that "Come" (or "Sit" or "Down") is a three- or four-word command.

2. Never correct your dog for something he did minutes earlier. Five seconds, remember?

Many types of plants and flowers can be toxic to dogs. Be sure your garden doesn't contain plants that can cause your Boxer harm.

3. Always praise (and treat) as soon as he does something good (or stops doing something naughty). How else will your puppy know he's a good dog?

4. Be consistent. You can't snuggle together on the couch to watch TV today, then scold him for climbing on the couch tomorrow.

5. Never tell your dog to "Come" and then correct him for something he did wrong. He will think the correction is for coming to you. (Think like a dog, remember?) Always go to the dog to stop unwanted behavior (*in the act,* remember?)

6. *Never* hit or kick your dog or strike him with a newspaper or other object. Such abusive measures will only create fear and confusion in your dog and could provoke aggressive behavior down the road.

7. When praising or correcting, use your best doggie voice. Use a light and happy voice for praise, and a firm, sharp voice for warnings or corrections. A pleading, whiny "No, No" or "Drop that" will not sound too convincing, nor will a deep, gruff voice

make your puppy feel like he's a good dog.

Your dog also will respond accordingly to family arguments. If there's a shouting match, he will think

PLAYING GAMES

Puppy games are a great way to entertain your puppy and yourself, while subliminally teaching lessons in the course of having fun. Start with a

Puppy catch-me begins as a game of chase with the littermates.

that he did something wrong and head for cover. So never argue in front of the kids...*or* the dog!

Despite the Boxer's powerful appearance, he is a soft dog who will not respond to harsh training methods or corrections. Puppy kindergarten and continued lessons in obedience are the best course to combating the Boxer stubborn streak.

game plan and a pocketful of tasty dog treats. Keep your games short so you don't push his attention span beyond normal Boxer puppy limits.

Puppy Catch-Me

This one helps teach the come command. With two people sitting on the floor about 10 or 15 feet apart, one person holds and pets the pup while the other calls him "Puppy, puppy, Come!" in a happy voice. When pup comes running to you, lavish him with big hugs and give a tasty treat. Repeat back and forth several times...don't overdo it.

You can add a ball or one of his favorite toys and toss it back and forth for puppy to retrieve. When he picks it up, praise and hug some more, give him a goodie to release the toy, then toss it back to person number two. Repeat as before.

Hide and Seek

This is another game that teaches "Come." Play this game outdoors in your yard or other enclosed safe area. When the pup is distracted, hide behind a tree. Peek out to see when he discovers you are gone and comes running back to find you (trust me, he will do that). As soon as he gets close, come out, squat down with arms outstretched and call him: "Puppy, Come!" This is also an excellent bonding aid and teaches puppy to depend on you.

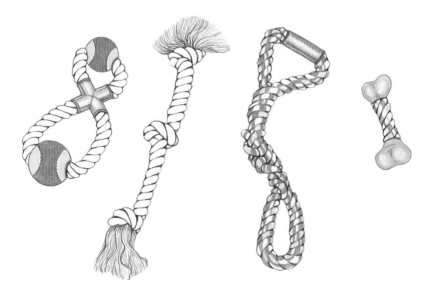

Visit your pet shop for fun interactive toys.

Where's Your Toy?

Start by placing one of your puppy's favorite toys in plain sight. Ask him "Where's your toy?" and let him take it. Then place your puppy safely outside the room and place the toy where only part of it shows. Bring him back and ask the same question. Praise highly when he finds it. Repeat several times. Finally, conceal the toy completely and let the puppy sniff it out. Trust his nose...he will find his toy.

Puppies love to have fun with their people. Giving them interactive games is the best way to train them. Games are excellent

"Find your toy." Your puppy will follow his nose every time!

teaching aids and one of the best ways to say "I love you" to your puppy.

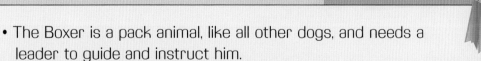

BOXER PUPPY KINDERGARTEN

Overview

- The Boxer is a pack animal, like all other dogs, and needs a leader to guide and instruct him.
- Positive reinforcement is the best way to train any dog, especially one as sensitive as the Boxer.
- Know the basic rules of puppy classes: you are "alpha" and your dog doesn't speak English.
- Teach word association, timing and consistency.
- Learn the seven rules to successful puppy training.
- Play games with your puppy to help him learn to come when called.

House-training Your Boxer

Young male puppies squat like females when they urinate. They outgrow this trait when their hormones start flowing around 16 to 20 weeks of age.

Successful house-training should be your primary focus after you bring your Boxer puppy home. Use your dog crate and common dog sense, and your pup will soon master the basics of potty-training. Canines are natural den creatures, thanks to the thousands of years their ancestors spent living in caves and holes in the ground, so puppies adapt quite naturally to crate confinement.

Puppies are also very clean by nature and hate to soil their dens or living spaces, which makes the crate a natural house-training aid. Thus, his crate is actually a multi-purpose dog accessory; it is your Boxer's personal dog house within your house, a humane house-training tool, a security measure that will protect your house and everything in it when you're not home, a travel aid to house and protect your dog when traveling (most motels will accept a crated dog) and, finally, a comfortable dog space for your puppy when your anti-dog relatives come to visit.

Your Boxer will want to frequent the same outside locations to relieve himself from day to day.

Some experienced breeders insist on crate use after their puppies leave, and a few even crate-train their pups before they send them home. It's more likely, though, that your Boxer has never seen a crate, so it's up to you to make sure his introduction is a pleasant one.

Introduce the crate as soon as he comes home so he learns that this is his new "house." For the first day or two, toss a tiny treat into the crate to entice him to go in. Pick a crate

Boxers are eager to learn from their owners. Be patient and fair and your puppy will heed your good example.

command, such as "Kennel," "Inside" or "Crate," and use it when he enters. You also can feed his first few meals inside the crate with the door still open, so the crate association will be a happy one.

Puppy should sleep in his crate from his very first night at home. He may whine or object to the confinement, but be strong and stay the course. If you release him when he cries, you provide his first life lesson…if I cry, I get out and maybe even hugged. Hmmm…not a good plan after all.

A better scheme is to place the crate next to your bed at night for the first few weeks. Your presence will comfort him, and you'll also know if he needs a middle-of-the-night potty trip. Whatever you do, do not lend comfort by taking puppy into bed with you. To a dog, being on the bed means that he is your equal, which is not a good idea this early in the game.

Make a practice of placing puppy in his crate for naps, at nighttime and whenever you are unable to watch him closely. Not to worry… he will let you know when he wakes up and needs a potty trip. If he falls asleep under the table and wakes up when you're not there, guess what he'll do first? Make a puddle, then walk over to say "Hi!"

Become a Boxer vigilante. Routines, consistency and an eagle eye are your keys to house-training success. Puppies always "go" when they wake up (quickly now!), after eating, after play periods and after brief periods of confinement. Most pups under 12 weeks of age will need to eliminate at least every hour or so, or up to 10 times a day. (Set your oven timer to remind you.)

Always take puppy outside to the same area, telling him "Outside" as you go out. Use your chosen potty command ("Hurry up," "Go Potty" and so forth) when he does his business, lavishing him with "Good puppy, Hurry up!" Always use the same exit door for these potty trips, and confine the puppy to the exit area so he can find it when he have a house map in his head.

Of course, he will have accidents. All puppies do. If you catch him in the act, clap your hands loudly, say "Aaah! Aaah!" and scoop him up to

Dogs hate to soil their dens (crates, for example). Give your pup the opportunity to visit the outdoors when Nature calls, and don't ignore the signs when he has "to go."

needs it. Watch for sniffing and circling, sure signs that he needs to relieve himself. Don't allow him to roam the house until he's fully house-trained...how will he find that outside door if he's three or four rooms away? He does not go outside. Your voice should startle him and make him stop...maybe. Be sure to praise the pup when he finishes his duty outside.

If you discover the piddle spot after the fact... more than five seconds later…you're too late. Dogs only understand in the moment and will not understand a correction given more than five seconds after the deed. Correcting any later than this will only cause fear and confusion. Just forget it and vow to be more vigilant.

Never (that is spelled N-E-V-E-R) rub your puppy's nose in his mistake or strike your puppy or adult dog with your hand, a newspaper or other object to correct him. He will not understand and will only become fearful of the person who is hitting him.

Potty hint: Remove puppy's water after 7 p.m. to aid in nighttime bladder control. If he gets thirsty, offer him an ice cube. Then just watch him race for the refrigerator when he hears the rattle of the ice cube tray.

Despite its many benefits, crate use can be abused. Puppies under 12 weeks of age should never be confined for more than two hours at a time, unless, of course, they are sleeping. A general rule of thumb is three hours maximum for a three-month old pup, four or five for the four- to five-month old, and no more than six hours for dogs over six months of age. If you're unable to be home to release the dog, arrange for a relative, neighbor or dog-sitter to let him out to exercise and potty.

If you are unable to use a crate for house-training, or prefer to paper-train your Boxer pup, the routine is basically the same. Assign an out-of-the-way elimination place and cover it with newspaper. Take your puppy to the designated papered area on schedule. Use the specified potty word, and praise when he does his business. Do not use the area for any other purpose except potty breaks. Keep the area clean. You can place a small piece of soiled paper on the clean ones to remind puppy why he's there. His nose will tell him what to do!

What to do with an uncrated puppy when you're not home? (Not a wise choice for a Boxer puppy.) Confine him to one area with a dog-proof barrier. Puppy-proofing alone may not be enough. An exercise pen 4 x 4 feet square (available through pet shops), sturdy enough that pup can't knock it down, will provide safe containment for short periods. Paper one area for elimination, with perhaps a blanket in the opposite corner for napping. Provide safe chew toys to keep him occupied, but even that is risky at best. If you don't or won't crate and cannot supervise your pup, be prepared to meet the consequences.

Most importantly, remember that successful house-training revolves around your consistent efforts to reach the goal. You must maintain a strict schedule and use your key words consistently. Well-trained owners have well-trained Boxer pups.

HOUSE-TRAINING YOUR BOXER

Overview

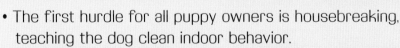

- The first hurdle for all puppy owners is housebreaking, teaching the dog clean indoor behavior.
- The crate is the best answer to house-training your Boxer. Learn how to use a crate, not abuse it.
- Teach a relief command so that your puppy will always indicate when he needs to go out.
- Control your puppy's water intake: what goes in...
- Paper training is an option for a Boxer puppy, though it is surely not as reliable as crate training.

Teaching Basic Commands

Despite the Boxer's stubborn streak, he is a bright student and quick to learn. You must be deliberate and patient, as harsh teaching methods will only cause the dog to balk and resist your efforts. Start his puppy lessons as soon as he comes home. Research has proven that the earlier you begin, the easier the process and the more successful you both will be. Always start your teaching exercises in a quiet, distraction-free environment. Once your Boxer pup

One person should set down the Boxer's training routine; he will progress to taking commands from all family members.

has mastered any task, change the setting and practice in a different location…another room, the yard, and then practice with another person or a dog nearby. If the pup reacts to the new distraction and does not perform the exercise, back up and continue with the exercise by going back to no distractions for a while.

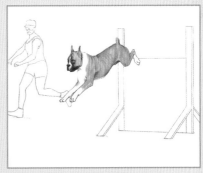

Once the basic commands are mastered, the Boxer knows no bounds in obedience! How about the high jump?

Appoint one person to instruct your puppy in the early stages so that your pup is not confused. It's the "too-many-cooks" rule of dog training. Once the puppy has learned a command reliably, other family members can join in.

Ignore your Boxer for a few minutes before each training session. (Just a few minutes, as Boxers do not like to be ignored.) The lack of stimulation will make him more eager for your company and attention.

Keep lessons short so your puppy won't get bored or lose his enthusiasm. This is especially important

Boxers are sensitive to being scolded, but a reprimand is called for whenever you catch the Boxer "in the act."

with a Boxer. In time, he will be able to concentrate for longer periods. Vary the exercises to keep his enthusiasm level high. Watch for signs of boredom and loss of attention.

Always keep your training sessions positive and upbeat. Use lots of praise, praise and more praise. Never train your puppy or adult dog if you are in a grumpy mood. You will lose patience, and he will think it is his fault. That will reverse any progress the two of you have made.

Finish every training session on a positive note. If you have been struggling or unsuccessful, switch gears and do something he knows well (Sit!) and end the session.

EARLY LESSON PLANS

Before you can effectively teach your puppy any command, two things must happen. Puppy must learn to respond to his name (name recognition), and you must be able to gain and hold his attention. How to accomplish that? Why, with treats, of course! Most Boxers live for food!

Treats are defined as tiny tidbits, preferably soft and easy to chew. You don't want to overfeed the pup. Thin slices of hot dogs cut in quarters work well.

Attention and Name Recognition

Start by calling your Boxer puppy's name. Once. Not two or three times, but once. Otherwise he will learn he has a three-part name and will ignore you when you say it once. Begin by using his name when he is undistracted and you know that he will look at you. Pop him a treat as soon as he looks at you. Repeat this at least a dozen times, several times a day. It won't take more than a day or so before he understands that his name means something good to eat.

Establish a Release Command

That's the word you'll use to tell him that the exercise is over, similar to "At ease" in the military. "All done" and "Free" are the ones most commonly recommended. You'll need a release word so your Boxer will know that it's okay to relax or move from a stationary position.

Take It and Leave It

This command offers too many advantages to list. Place a treat in the palm of your hand and tell your pup to "Take it" as he grabs the treat. Repeat three times. On the fourth time, do not say a word when your pup reaches for the treat...just close your fingers around the treat and wait. Do not pull away, but be prepared for the pup to paw, lick, bark and nibble on your fingers. When he finally pulls away from your hand, usually in puzzlement, open your hand and tell him "Take it."

Now, the next step. Show your Boxer the treat in the palm of your hand and tell him to "Leave it." When he goes for the treat, close your

Maintain your Boxer's focus. Tell him "Leave it" when he wants to chew on a broken branch.

hand, repeat "Leave it." Repeat the process until he pulls away, wait just a second, then open your hand and tell him to "Take it." Repeat "Leave it" until he waits just a few seconds, then give the treat on "Take it." Gradually extend the time you wait when puppy leaves it on command, and before you tell him "Take it."

Now you want to teach your dog to leave things on the ground, not just in your hand. (Think of all the things you don't want him to pick up.) Position yourself in front of your dog, and toss a treat behind you and a little to the side so he can see the treat, and tell him to "Leave it." Here begins the dance. If he goes for the treat, use your body, not your hands, to block him, moving him backwards away from it. As soon as he backs off and gives up trying to get around you, unblock the treat and tell him "Take it." Be ready to block again if he goes for it before you give permission. Repeat the process until he under-stands and waits for the command.

Once your Boxer knows this well, practice with his food dish, telling him to "Leave it," then "Take it" after he complies (he can either sit or stand while waiting for his dish). As before, gradually extend the waiting period before you tell him "Take it."

This little training exercise sends many messages to your Boxer. He is reminded that you're the boss, that all good things, like food, come from his lord and master (or lady and mistress!). It will help prevent your puppy from becoming too possessive of his food bowl, a behavior that only escalates and leads to more serious aggressive behaviors. The benefits of a solid "Take it/Leave it" are endless.

Come Command

This command has life-saving potential…preventing your Boxer from running into the street, going after a squirrel, chasing a child on a bike, the list goes on and on.

Always practice this command on leash. You can't afford to risk failure, or your pup will learn that he does not have to come when called. Once you have the pup's attention, call him from a short distance with "Puppy, Come!" (use your happy voice!) and give a treat when he comes to you. If he hesitates, tug him to you gently with his leash. Grasp and hold his collar with one hand as you dispense the treat. This is important. You will eventually phase out the treat and switch to hands-on praise. This maneuver also connects holding his collar with coming and treating, which will assist you in countless future behaviors. Do 10 or 12 repetitions 2 or 3 times a day. Once pup has mastered the come command, continue to practice daily to engrave this most important behavior into his tiny brain. Experienced Boxer owners know, however, that you can never completely trust a dog to come when called if the dog is bent on a self-appointed

mission. "Off-leash" is often synonymous with "out of control."

Sit Command

This one's a snap, since your Boxer already understands the treating process. Stand in front of your pup, move the treat directly over his nose and slowly move it backwards. As he folds backwards to reach the goodie, his rear will move downward to the floor If the puppy raises up to reach the treat, just lower it a bit. The

Sit is a natural position for a dog. Teach this command first.

CHAPTER 9

moment his behind touches the floor, tell him "Sit." (That's one word…"Sit.") Release the treat and gently grasp that collar as you did with "Come." He will again make that positive connection between the treat, the sit position and the collar hold.

As time goes by, make him hold the sit position longer before you treat (this is the beginning of the stay

You can go from the sit to the sit-stay exercise fairly easily. The stay exercise is very important as it can save the dog's life in emergency situations.

command). Start using your release word to release him from the sit position. Practice using the "Sit" command for everyday activities, such as sitting for his food bowl or a toy. Do random sits

throughout the day, always for a food or praise reward. Once he is reliable, combine the "Sit" and "Leave it" for his food dish. Your pup is expanding his vocabulary.

Stay Command

"Stay" is really just an extension of "Sit," which your Boxer already knows. With puppy sitting when commanded, place the palm of your hand in front of his nose and tell him "Stay." Count to five. Give him his release word to leave the stay position and praise. Stretch out the stays in tiny incre-ments…making allowances for puppy energy. Once he stays reliably, take one step backwards, then forward again. Gradually extend the time and distance that you move away. If puppy moves from his stay position, say "No" and move forward in front of him. Use sensible timelines depending on your puppy's attention span.

Down Command

Down can be a tough command to master. Because the down is a submissive posture, take-charge breeds like Boxers may find it especially difficult. That's why it's most important to teach it when they're very young.

From the sit position, move the food lure from his nose to the ground and slightly backwards between his front paws. Wiggle it as necessary. As soon as his front legs and rear end hit the floor, give the treat and tell him "Down, Good boy, Down!" thus connecting the word to the behavior. Be patient, and be generous with the praise when he cooperates.

Once he goes into the down position with ease, incorporate the stay command as you did with sit. By six months of age, the puppy should be able to do a solid sit-stay for ten minutes, ditto for a down-stay.

The down command is the most challenging command to teach a dominant dog like the Boxer.

Once the dog is down, reward him with a treat.

Hold another treat in your hand, but don't release it. Just pet him and offer encouraging words and praise.

Heel Command

The actual heel command comes a bit later in the learning curve. A young Boxer should be taught simply to walk politely on a leash, at or near your side. That is best accomplished when your pup is very young and small, instead of 30 or 40 pounds pulling you down the street.

Start leash training as

soon as pup comes home. Simply attach it to his buckle collar and let him drag it around for a little while every day. If he chews his leash, distract him with play activities or spray the leash with a product made to deter chewing, which will make it taste unpleasant. Play a game with the leash on.

After a few days, gather up

Your dog must learn to heel properly so you can walk together without his pulling you or dragging behind.

the leash in a distraction-free zone…house or yard… and take just a few steps together. Hold a treat lure at your side to encourage the puppy to walk next to you. Pat your knee and use a happy voice. Move forward just a few steps each time. Say "Let's go!"

when you move forward, hold the treat to keep him near, take a few steps, give the treat and praise!

Keep these sessions short and happy, a mere 30 seconds at a time. Never scold or nag him into walking faster or slower, just encourage him with happy talk. Walk straight ahead at first, adding wide turns once he gets the hang of it. Progress to 90-degree turns, using a gentle leash tug, a happy verbal "Let's go!" and, of course, a treat. Walk in short 30- to 40-second bursts, with a happy break (use your release word) and brief play (hugs will do nicely) in between. Keep total training time short and always quit with success, even if just a few short steps.

Wait

You'll love this one, especially when your Boxer comes in the house with wet or muddy paws. Work on the wait command with a closed door.

Start to open the door as if to go through or out. When your dog tries to follow, step in front and body-block him to prevent his passage. Don't use the wait command just yet. Keep it up until he gives up and you can open the door a little to pass through. Then say "Through" or "Okay" and let him go through the door. Repeat by body-blocking until he understands and waits for you, then start applying the "Wait" to the behavior. Practice in different doorways inside your home, using outside entrances (to safe or enclosed areas) only after he will wait reliably.

Keep Practicing

Ongoing practice in obedience is actually a lifetime dog rule, especially for a strong-willed Boxer. Dogs will be dogs, and, if we don't maintain their skills, they will sink back into sloppy, inattentive behaviors that will be harder to correct. Incorporate these commands into your daily routine, and your dog will remain a gentleman you can be proud of.

TEACHING BASIC COMMANDS

Overview

- Begin basic obedience training on the right paw: select a quiet (distraction-free) environment; decide who will be the one person who trains the dog; and keep lessons short and positive.
- Get your puppy's attention and maintain it.
- Teach name recognition and establish a release command.
- Two easy lessons: "Take it" and "Leave it" prove versatile and helpful.
- The basic commands include come, sit, stay, down, heel and wait.
- Practice with your Boxer daily so that he becomes consistent 100% of the time.

Home Care for Your Boxer

You are responsible for the long-term quality of your Boxer's life. You are his dietitian, dentist, personal trainer and home health-care provider. Your dog will depend on you in sickness and in health. The more you know about canine health, the better prepared you'll be to handle everyday health issues and emergencies.

Of all the regimens included in this chapter, two are, without question, the most important…weight control and dental hygiene. Veterinarians tell us that over 50% of the dogs they examine are grossly overweight, and that such

By spending time with your Boxer every day, you will always recognize the signs of good health.

obesity will take two to three years off a dog's life, given the strain it puts on the animal's heart, joints and vital organs. The message here is obvious: lean is healthier.

To determine if your Boxer is overweight, you should be able to feel your dog's ribs beneath a thin layer of muscle with very gentle pressure on his rib cage. When viewing your dog from above, you should be able to see a definite waistline; from the side, he should have an obvious tuck-up in his abdomen.

In the warm months, you must keep your Boxer cool and relaxed. Heat stroke is a common emergency in the summertime.

Keep a record of his weight from each annual vet visit. A few extra pounds? Adjust his food portions (eliminate those table scraps), perhaps switch to a "light," "senior" or lower-calorie dog food formula and increase his exercise.

Excessive weight is especially hard on older dogs with creaky joints. A senior Boxer who is sedentary will

The puppy's frame should not carry too much excess weight, basically appearing like an adult in miniature.

become out of shape more quickly. Walking and running (slower for old guys) are still the best workouts for health maintenance. Tailor your dog's exercise to fit his age and physical condition.

Now that your dog is slim and trim, let's examine his teeth. The American Veterinary Dental Society states that by age three, 80% of dogs exhibit signs of gum disease. (Quick, look at your dog's teeth!) Symptoms include yellow and brown build-up of tartar along the gumline, red, inflamed gums and persistent bad breath. If neglected, these conditions will allow bacteria to accumulate in your dog's mouth and enter your dog's bloodstream through those damaged gums, increasing the risk for disease in vital organs such as the heart, liver and kidneys. It's also known that periodontal disease is a major contributor to kidney disease, which is a common cause of death in older dogs...and is highly preventable.

Your vet should examine your Boxer's teeth and gums during his annual checkup to make sure they are clean and healthy. He may recommend professional cleaning if there is excessive plaque build-up.

During the other 364 days of the year, you are your dog's dentist. Brush his teeth daily, or at least twice a week. Use a doggie toothbrush (designed for the contour of a canine's mouth) and use dog toothpaste, which is flavored with chicken, beef and liver. (Minty human toothpaste is harmful to dogs.) If your dog resists a toothbrush, try a washcloth or gauze pad wrapped around your finger. Start the brushing process with gentle gum massages when your pup is very young so he will learn to tolerate and even enjoy the process.

Feeding dry dog food is an excellent way to help minimize plaque accumulation. You can also treat your dog to hard dog biscuits and a raw carrot every day. Carrots help scrub away plaque while providing extra vitamins A and C. Invest in healthy chew objects, such as rubber bones and toys with ridges that act as tartar scrapers. Beef knuckle bones (raw, not cooked, which splinter) also work, but watch for sharp corners and splintering on any chew object, which can cut the dog's mouth and can damage his intestinal lining if pieces are swallowed.

Your weekly grooming sessions should include body checks for lumps (cysts, warts and fatty tumors), hot spots and other skin or coat problems. Rub your dog down with your hands; don't rely on the brush to find abnormalities. Although harmless lumps under the skin are common in older dogs, many can be malignant, and your · vet should examine any abnormality. Black mole-like patches or growths on any body part, especially between the toes, require immediate veterinary inspection. Remember, petting and

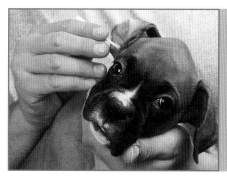

Never use a cotton swab to clean the Boxer's ears. A soft wipe or cotton ball is best to cleanse the outer ear; never probe into the ear canal.

hugging can also reveal little abnormalities.

Be extra-conscious of dry skin, a flaky coat and thinning hair, all signs of thyroid disease. Check for fleas and flea dirt if you think fleas may be present. Have annual stool cultures done to check for intestinal parasites...hook, whip and roundworms can cause poor coat quality and all manner of intestinal problems, and can weaken your dog's resistance to other canine diseases.

Check your Boxer's ears

weekly…are they clean and fresh-smelling? Have your vet show you the proper way to clean them. Remember too, many old dogs grow deaf with age. Sure, a smart dog can develop selective hearing and sometimes will not "hear" you, but you'll know it's a true hearing deficit when he no longer hears the clinking of the cookie jar. Time and experience will show you what changes and allowances to make if your dog develops hearing loss.

Your Boxer's vision also may deteriorate with age. A bluish haze is common in geriatric dogs and does not impair vision. Always check with your vet about any change in the eyes to determine if it's a problem.

How about his other end…does he chew at his rear or scoot and rub it on the carpet? That's a sign of impacted anal glands. Have your vet express those glands (it's not a job for amateurs).

Heart disease is common in all canines, and Boxers are prone, yet it is one problem that dog owners most frequently overlook. Symptoms include panting and shortness of breath, chronic coughing, especially at night or upon first waking in the morning, and changes in sleeping habits. Cardiomyopathy may also cause "fainting" spells and fluid retention in the abdomen. Many forms of heart disease can be treated if caught early.

Kidney disease also can be treated successfully with early diagnosis. Dogs seven years old and older should be tested annually for healthy kidney and liver function. If your dog drinks excessive amounts of water, urinates more frequently or has accidents in the house, run, don't walk, to your vet. Kidney failure can be managed with special diets to reduce the workload on the kidneys.

The moral here is: Know your Boxer! Early detection is

the key to your dog's longevity and quality of life.

For everyday common-sense care, every dog owner should know the signs of an emergency. Many dog agencies, humane societies and animal shelters sponsor canine first-aid seminars. Participants learn how to recognize and deal with signs of common emergency situations, how to assemble a first-aid kit and how to give CPR to a dog.

Obvious emergencies include vomiting for more than 24 hours, bloody or prolonged (over 24 hours) diarrhea, fever (normal canine temperature is 101.5°F) and a sudden swelling of the head or any body part (allergic reaction to an insect bite or other stimulus). Symptoms of other common emergency situations include: heatstroke, hypothermia and shock.

Visit your veterinarian at once if you notice any of these warning signs. Many canine diseases are treatable if diagnosed in the early stages.

HOME CARE FOR YOUR BOXER

Overview

- Weight control and dental care should be foremost on every Boxer owner's home-care routine. Obesity can shorten the life of your Boxer, as can plaque accumulation (and the diseases associated with it).
- During weekly grooming sessions, keep an eye on the condition of your Boxer's coat. Always watch for moles, bumps, lumps and parasites, all of which can lead to serious problems.
- Know the signs of wellness so that you can recognize when your Boxer's health may be compromised by disease.

BOXER

Feeding Your Boxer

When planning a feeding program for your Boxer puppy, it's best to think "quality" and not "economy." The poor nutritional quality of some of the cheaper dog foods do not provide a fully digestible product nor do they contain the proper balance of the vitamins, minerals and fatty acids necessary to support healthy muscle, skin and coat. Canine nutrition research also has proven that you have to feed larger quantities of a cheaper food to maintain proper body. To keep your Boxer in prime condition, feed a

Feed your Boxer puppy a sensible, balanced diet to promote proper growth and weight gain during his crucial development period.

quality dog food that is appropriate for his age and lifestyle. Ask your vet to make recommendations.

Premium dog-food manufacturers have developed their formulas with strict quality controls, using only quality ingredients obtained from reliable sources. The labels on the food bags tell you what products are in the food (beef, chicken, corn, etc.), with ingredients listed in descending order of weight or amount in the food. Do not add your own supplements, "people food" or extra vitamins to the food. You will only upset the nutritional balance of the food, which could affect the growth pattern of your Boxer pup.

In the world of quality dog foods, there are enough choices to confuse even experienced dog folks. The major brands now offer foods for every size, age and activity level. As with human infants, puppies require a diet different than that of an adult. The new growth

There is nothing inexpensive about first-quality dog food! Discuss the best brand with your chosen breeder.

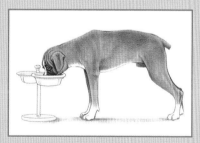

Use elevated food and water bowls so that your Boxer will be able to feed more safely and comfortably.

formulas contain protein and fat levels that are appropriate for different-sized breeds. Large-breed, fast-growing dogs require less protein and fat during their early months of rapid growth, which is better for healthy joint development. Accordingly, medium (your Boxer) breeds also have different nutritional requirements during their first year of growth.

Don't be intimidated by all those dog food bags on the store shelves. Read the labels on the bags. Ask your breeder and your vet what food they recommend for your Boxer pup. A solid education in the dog-food business will provide the tools you need to offer your dog a diet that is best for his long-term health.

If you plan to switch from the food fed by your breeder, take home a small supply of the breeder's food to mix with your own to aid your puppy's adjustment to his new food.

When and how much to feed? An eight-week-old puppy does best eating three times a day. (Tiny tummies, tiny meals.) At about 12 weeks of age, you can switch to twice-daily feeding. Most breeders suggest two meals a day during the life of the dog, regardless of breed. This is especially important for the Boxer. Smaller, more frequent meals also help prevent the possibility of bloat, as some theories suggest that gulping large amounts of food or drinking copious amounts of water right after eating can contribute to the condition.

Other bloat-prevention measures include no heavy exercise for at least an hour before eating and two hours afterwards. Make sure your dog is not overly excited during meals. It is also believed that nervous and overly excited dogs are more prone to this life-threatening condition. As previously mentioned, elevate your Boxer's food and water bowls.

Free feeding, that is, leaving a bowl of food available all day, is not recommended. Free feeding fosters picky eating habits…a bite here, a nibble there. Free feeders also are more likely to become possessive of their food bowls, a problem behavior that signals the beginning of resource guarding and aggression. Scheduled meals remind your Boxer that all good things come from his owner.

With scheduled meals, it's also easier to predict elimination, which is the better road to house-training. Regular meals help you know just how much puppy eats and when, plus it provides valuable information about your pup's health (changes in his eating habits can signal a problem).

Like people, puppies and adult dogs have different appetites; some will eat and lick their food bowls clean and beg for more, while others pick at their food and leave some of it untouched. If

WAYS TO WARD OFF BLOAT

Owners should take precautions to protect their dogs from the possible onset of bloat. Here are some commonsense steps to avoid your dog swallowing air while he's eating or upsetting his digestion:

- Buy top-quality dog food that is high nutrition/low residue. Test the kibble in a glass of water. If it swells up to four times its original size, try another brand.

- Purchase a bowl stand to elevate your dog's food and water bowls. Dogs should not crane their necks when they are eating.

- No exercise one hour before and after all meals.

- Never allow your dog to gulp his food or water. Feed him when he is calm.

- Place large unswallowable objects in his bowl to prevent him from "inhaling" his food in two mouthfuls.

the puppy is properly exercised, offering a little extra food is recommended. Chubby puppies may be cute and cuddly, but the extra weight could stress their growing joints. It also may be a factor in the development of hip and elbow disease.

Proud owner Joey Agnello with his two Boxers, Chelsea and Durante. Joey was one of the many New York firefighters killed in the Twin Towers on September 11, 2001.

Overweight pups also tend to grow into overweight adults, who are more susceptible to other health problems.

Always remember that lean is healthy, fat is not, especially for adults. Obesity is a major canine killer. Quite simply, a lean dog lives longer than one who is overweight. Furthermore, think of the better quality of life for the lean dog who can run, jump and play without the burden of an extra 10 or 20 pounds.

Should you feed canned or dry food? Should you offer the dry food with or without water? Dry food is recommended by most vets, since the dry particles help clean the dog's teeth of plaque and tartar. Adding water to dry food is optional. A bit of water added immediately before eating is thought to enhance the flavor of the food while still preserving the dental benefits. Whether feeding wet or dry, always have drinking water available at all times, keeping in mind that large amounts of water at mealtimes and gulping water are not good for your Boxer.

To complicate the dog-food dilemma, there are also raw foods available for those who prefer to feed their dogs a completely natural diet rather than traditional manufactured dog food. The debate on raw and/or all-natural vs. manufactured is a fierce one, with the raw-food proponents claiming that raw diets have cured their dog's allergies and other chronic ailments. Check with your vet and ask your breeder.

If your adult dog is overweight, you can switch to a "light" food, which has fewer calories and more fiber. "Senior" foods for older dogs have formulas designed to meet the needs of less active, older dogs. "Performance" diets contain more fat and protein for dogs that compete in sporting disciplines or lead very active lives.

The bottom line is this: What and how much you feed your dog are major factors in his overall health and longevity. It's worth your investment in extra time and dollars to determine the best diet for your Boxer. This will pay off in a longer and happier life for you and your Boxer.

FEEDING YOUR BOXER

Overview

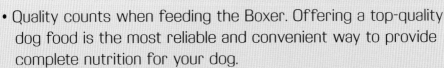

- Quality counts when feeding the Boxer. Offering a top-quality dog food is the most reliable and convenient way to provide complete nutrition for your dog.
- Discuss with your vet and/or breeder the amount to feed your Boxer.
- Avoid free feeding, which can lead to picky eaters, obesity or possessive behavior.
- Bloat is a life-threatening condition that affects deep-chested dogs. It is related to eating and feeding habits.
- Your Boxer's health relies upon a proper diet.

CHAPTER 12

Grooming Your Boxer

The Boxer's short, close-lying coat requires minimal upkeep, so grooming your Boxer is a simple task. But grooming involves more than just brushing your dog. It also includes his ears, teeth and nails, and a thorough body check for external parasites, wounds, lumps and bumps. Good grooming habits are an essential part of your Boxer's overall health-care program and should be a weekly routine all year long.

Every dog should enjoy the hands-on grooming process; it's the next best

The short coat of the Boxer requires only limited brushing. A rubber curry brush makes an ideal tool for the puppy.

thing to petting. To that end, the brush, nail clippers and toothbrush are best introduced when your Boxer is just a pup. Some dogs who have not experienced these ministrations may object when they are older...*and bigger*...and better able to resist. Grooming will then become a distasteful chore, even a battle, rather than a routine procedure that both of you can enjoy. The lesson here...*start young.*

Hold your first grooming session as soon as your puppy has adjusted to his new home. Start with tiny increments of time, stroking him gently with a soft brush, briefly handling his paws, looking inside his ears, gently touching his gums. Use lots of sweet talk and offer little bits of dog treats during each session, so he'll think such personal contact is a prelude to a feast. Ah, the power of positive association!

The Boxer coat is virtually groom-free. He has no thick undercoat, so

Virtually maintenance-free, Boxers thrive on quality time with their owners.

The best way to trim the nails is with a nail grinder, set on a low speed. This avoids ever cutting the quick.

shedding is not a problem as with long-haired breeds. His short coat requires little more than a weekly brushing with a rubber curry used for horses then a soft bristle brush to remove dust and loose hair. A rub-down with a chamois leather or a hound mitt (a rubber grooming glove) also works very well.

Because Boxers are so clean and groom themselves, frequent bathing is seldom necessary, and, in fact, will remove the essential oils that keep your dog's skin supple and his coat soft and gleaming. Frequent brushing is the best way to give his coat a super sheen.

Of course, there are those times when a bath is necessary. Bathing rituals can be a challenge if your dog dislikes water or getting lathered up. To minimize the stress and struggle of bath time, start when your pup is small. Imagine wrestling a 60- or 70-pound adult into the tub or shower stall. Lure your puppy into the tub with the usual food rewards; perhaps enhance him with a tiny bit of tasty stuff like soft cheese or peanut butter to turn your tub into a buffet table.

Because of their short coats, Boxers are easily chilled. They should be thoroughly dried and kept away from drafts after bathing and drying to prevent chilling.

Nails should be trimmed twice a month. This is always the least favorite grooming chore, and the one most often neglected. Early introduction will help make the clipping process easier. Puppies do not naturally like pedicures, so start nail clipping as soon as possible. Offer those puppy treats with each clipping lesson. Thus, puppy will learn that when you touch his paws or trim those nails, he will receive a food reward.

At first, you may have to settle on only one or two nails at a time to avoid a boxing match. It is better to trim a small amount of nail more frequently than to try to cut back a nail that has grown too long. Nip off the nail tip or clip at the curved part of the nail. Be careful not to cut the quick (the pink vein in the nail), as that is quite painful and may cause the nail to bleed profusely. You can staunch the bleeding with a few drops of a clotting solution, available from your vet or local drug store.

A Boxer with cropped ears is not as prone to ear infections and hematomas as is a Boxer with natural ears. However, weekly ear checks are still a necessity, as ear infections can occur in all dogs. Regular cleansing with a specially formulated ear cleanser will keep your dog's ears clean and odor-free.

Symptoms of ear infection include redness and/or swelling of the outer or inner ear, a nasty odor or dark, waxy discharge. If your dog digs at his ear(s) with his paw, shakes his head a lot or appears to lose his balance, see your vet at once.

GROOMING YOUR BOXER

Overview

- While the Boxer is a virtually groom-free dog, proper coat maintenance is a vital part of his overall health-care program and must be initiated when the pup is young.
- The Boxer owner must tend to his dog's coat as well as nails and ears.
- You will only have to bathe your Boxer occasionally, probably two or three times per year.
- When dealing with ear problems, owners must not wait too long to seek treatment and always must follow through with the medication for its entire prescribed course.

Keeping the Boxer Active

Exercise is a major component in your Boxer's health-care plan. Lively backyard play activities and on-leash walks will keep him mentally and physically fit. As with all breeds of dog, your Boxer should never be allowed to run loose except in fenced-in areas. Running at-large presents a danger to the dog and neighborhood.

That said, a long, brisk daily walk is important for your Boxer's well-being. How long and how far depends on your dog's age and physical condition, although most Boxers have

The Boxer willingly accepts as much (or as little) exercise as you offer him.

great endurance and could probably out-walk their owners.

A young Boxer's bones are relatively soft and his growth plates do not fully close until about 14 months of age. Thus, his musculo-skeletal structure is more vulnerable to injury during that period and should not be subjected to heavy stress. That means shorter walks at intervals throughout the day, and no games that encourage twisting, high jumping or heavy impact on his front or rear. Playtime with other puppies and older dogs also should be super-vised to avoid wrestling and twisting until your pup is past the danger age. Swimming, whenever possible, is an excellent form of exercise.

The more quality time you spend with your Boxer, the stronger will be his bond to you.

When and where to walk is as important as how long. On warm days, avoid walking during midday heat. Go out during the cooler morning or evening hours. If you are a jogger, your adult Boxer buddy is

Nothing keeps a Boxer as active as another Boxer.

the perfect running companion. Jogging on turf or other soft surface is easier on your Boxer's joints and feet. Just make sure your dog is fully developed, in good condition and up to doing your mile-plus run.

Those daily walks are also excellent bonding sessions. Your Boxer will look forward to his special time with you.

Boxers enjoy sports, especially "Monday Night Football" with a lady friend.

As a creature of habit, your dog will bounce with joy when he sees you don your cap, pick up his leash or rattle your house or car keys.

You can take your exercise program to another level. Plan a weekly night out with your Boxer and enroll in a class. Obedience, maybe agility...or both! The benefits of an obedience class are endless. You will be motivated to work with your dog daily so you won't look unprepared or unraveled at each week's class. Your dog will have a grand old time, and so will you. You'll both be more active, and thus healthier. Your dog will learn the basics of obedience, will be better behaved and will become a model citizen. He will discover that you really are the boss, and you will rule his dog world from that pedestal.

Agility class offers even more healthy outlets for an active Boxer. He will learn to scale an A-frame ramp, race headlong through a tunnel, balance himself on a teeter-totter, jump up and off a platform, jump through a hoop and zig-zag between a line of posts. The challenge of learning to navigate these agility obstacles, and his success in mastering each one, will make you proud of both of you! Agility training should not begin until the pup has completed his development phase.

You can take both of these activities one step further and show your dog in obedience and agility competition. Shows and trials are held year-round and are designed for all levels of experience. Find a club or join a training group. Working with other fanciers will give you the incentive to keep working with your dog. Check the American Boxer Club and AKC websites for details and contact people.

Conformation is by far the most popular canine competition for all breeds. If you plan to show your Boxer, make sure you start with a show-quality puppy and discuss your goals with the breeder. Most local breed clubs host conformation training classes and can help a novice get started. As with other competitions, it's best to start when he is young so he develops a good "ring" attitude.

KEEPING THE BOXER ACTIVE

Overview

- Structure an exercise regimen for your Boxer, allowing him daily walks and free running time in a safely enclosed area.
- Do not let young puppies exert themselves as they are more prone to injury at a young age.
- Do not overdo exercise on warm days.
- Daily walks reinforce that special bond between you and your Boxer.
- Additionally, consider enrolling in an obedience class to give your Boxer another fun outlet.
- Participating in dog shows, obedience and agility trials are excellent forums for dog and owner.

Your Boxer and His Vet

Author Rick Tomita examines a pup's ear at his Jacquet Kennel.

The veterinarian is a very important figure in your family's life. Your vet not only will help keep your Boxer healthy but also will help you become a better canine health-care provider.

Take your puppy to your veterinarian of choice within three or four days of bringing your puppy home. Show the vet any health records of shots and wormings from your breeder. The vet will conduct a thorough physical exam to make sure your Boxer is in good health, and work out a schedule for vaccinations, microchipping, routine medications and regular puppy visits. A good vet will be gentle and affectionate with a new pup and do everything possible to make sure the puppy is neither frightened nor intimidated.

Only a qualified vet should administer shots and medications to your pup.

Vaccine protocol varies with many veterinarians, but most recommend a series of three "combination" shots given at three- to four-week intervals. Your puppy should have had his first shot before he left his breeder.

"Combination" shots vary, and a single injection may contain five, six, seven or even eight vaccines in one shot. Many vets feel the potency in high-combination vaccines can negatively compromise a puppy's immature immune system. They recommend fewer vaccines in one shot or even separating vaccines into individual injections.

The wisest and most conservative course is to administer only one shot in a single visit, rather than two or

Like your children, your Boxer depends on you for his continued good health and happiness.

three shots at the same time.

The vaccines most commonly recommended by the American Veterinary Medical Association are those that protect against the most dangerous diseases, including distemper, canine parvovirus, canine hepatitis and rabies. Immunization is required in all 50 states. Vaccines no longer routinely recommended by the AVMA, except when the risk is present, are canine parainfluenza, leptospirosis, canine coronavirus, bordetella (kennel cough) and Lyme disease (canine borreliosis).

Heartworm is a problem that concerns dog owners. This is a worm that propagates inside your dog's heart and will ultimately kill him. Now found in all 50 states, heartworm is delivered through a mosquito bite. Heartworm preventative is a prescription medication available only through your veterinarian.

Of course, every dog owner faces flea and tick control. Fortunately, today there are several low-toxic, effective flea weapons to aid you in your flea war. Discuss the most up-to-date treatments with your vet.

Lyme disease, ehrlichiosis and Rocky Mountain spotted fever are tick-borne diseases now found in almost every state and can affect humans as well as dogs. Dogs that live in or visit areas where ticks are present, whether seasonally or year-round, must be protected. Over-the-counter flea and tick collars offer only limited protection.

All Boxer owners should know that Boxers have a serious reaction to a tranquilizing drug called Acepromazine. "Ace" is a pre-anesthetic frequently used before surgery. It has been shown to cause a serious arrhythmia of the heart when administered to some Boxers. This drug is also commonly prescribed as an oral tranquilizer for dogs traveling by car or air. If your Boxer ever needs a surgical procedure or tranquilizer, be sure to discuss with your vet which drugs will be used.

Your Boxer's health is in your hands between those annual visits to the vet. Be ever conscious of any changes in his appearance or behavior. Things to consider:

Has your Boxer gained a few too many pounds or suddenly lost weight? Are his teeth clean and white or does he need some plaque treatment? Is he urinating more frequently, drinking more water than usual? Does he strain during a bowel movement? Any changes in his appetite? Does he appear short of breath, lethargic, overly tired? Have you noticed limping or any sign of joint stiffness? These are all signs of serious health problems and you should discuss them with your

veterinarian as soon as they appear. This is especially important for the senior dog, since even a subtle change can be a sign of something serious.

Boxers love to interface with their owners, especially if the mistress is amenable to some kissing.

Spay/Neuter

Should you or shouldn't you? This is a question that concerns every Boxer owner. Many people believe that spaying or neutering your dog can save his life, though this is not true with the Boxer. The author has had many breeding males and females who remained whole (unaltered) for their whole lives with no ill effects whatsoever. Nevertheless, if you are keeping a Boxer solely as a companion and guard, neutering/spaying remains an excellent choice as it does relieve the owner of many of the complications associated with unaltered dogs. Male dogs who remain whole tend to wander away from home in search of a bitch in heat, and lift their legs on bushes and shrubs to mark their territory. Only males who have been bred may mark furniture indoors. Likewise, females go through their twice-annual estrus periods, which can be messy and problematic to owners. Certainly unwanted pregnancies are another disadvantage of keeping unaltered dogs. The decision, finally, rests with the owner, who should discuss the matter with his breeder and veterinarian.

YOUR BOXER AND HIS VET

Overview

- Upon bringing your Boxer home, take him to the vet for an exam.
- Discuss a vaccination schedule with your vet.
- Heartworm threatens the lives of dogs though it can be prevented through a prescription drug.
- Parasites like ticks and fleas can lead to various diseases that must be guarded against.
- Avoid the anesthetic Acepromazine for your Boxer.
- Keep a close eye on your Boxer's abnormal behavior for signs of potential problems.